FOLLOW HIS WAY

SCOTT A. HIGHFIELD

ISBN 979-8-88943-154-1 (paperback)
ISBN 979-8-88943-155-8 (digital)

Christian Faith Publishing
832 Park Avenue
Meadville, PA 16335
www.christianfaithpublishing.com

Printed in the United States of America

1

It was late spring in a small midwestern town named Margaret, with a population of 217. Margaret was a farming community with mostly grain farms, but there were still a few dairies left in the area. Supposedly, the town was named after an early pioneer's daughter who had died of a fever on the family's way west. Legend has it that she was buried on a small rise just north of the present town, and her parents were so grief-stricken they chose their home here. Thus, the town was born.

Zeb Walee had lived here all of his life, now working two jobs to support his wife, Janie, and the soon-to-be-218th resident of Margaret. Zeb was about six feet tall and was all muscle. His father was killed in a farming accident when he was small, and his mother passed away from cancer when he was a senior in high school. Zeb was an only child, so he was on his own. He worked eight hours a day at Morton's Garage repairing everything from bicycles to semis. In the evenings, he worked four hours loading rail cars at the Brice Brother's Grain Mill.

Janie grew up as Jane Sue Hupp in a town called Leets, the big city, with a population of 404, about twenty miles north of Margaret. It was here at Leets Elementary School where she first saw Zeb as they entered the kindergarten classroom. Zeb noticed her too! Who could have missed her? She had fiery red hair and a smile a mile wide. They sat next to each other and have been inseparable ever since. Janie's parents divorced right after she finished college, and they moved to different parts of the country. The only time she heard from them is when they needed something. She had an older brother, Martin, who left home when he turned eighteen, never to be heard from again.

Janie and Zeb had each other and not much more. They decided to get married in a small ceremony at a little church on the edge of town officiated by Pastor Ted Blakely. Pastor Blakely was in his early seventies, and he was well educated in books and in life. He made the young couple see how their life had been guided by God by putting them in each other's life many years earlier. He planted the seed of faith, hope, and love into their hearts, and that seed took root.

Janie was just finishing her first year of teaching, and she was six months along with their first baby. The baby would be here about the time school started in the fall. They had decided she would be a stay-at-home mom, but they weren't sure how they would pay their bills. Zeb always said, "God won't let us starve, so we will put our faith in Him, and it will be okay."

Shortly after school had finished for the summer, a customer in Morton's Garage asked, "Zeb, do you know anything about boilers?"

Zeb replied, "I ran Mr. Watkin's steam traction engine at the county fair, threshing wheat a couple of times."

"Well, I heard that Mercy General Hospital was looking for a boiler operator, and with your mechanical ability, you would be good at it! Plus, it would be a whole lot more money in your pocket. You should give it some thought."

"I will!" said Zeb.

That night at the supper table, Zeb brought up the subject to Janie. "I heard from a customer at the garage today that Mercy General Hospital is looking for a boiler operator, and I thought about applying for the job."

Her response was quick. "Do you know anything about boilers? Is it dangerous? How far of a drive is it?"

His answer was the same for all three questions. "I don't know, but I want to find out more. It will mean more money, which we can sure use. I think I will drive over there tomorrow and check in to it."

The next day, Zeb drove over to Mercy General Hospital. He inquired at the front desk about the open position and was instructed on how to get into the human resources department. There, he met a man in his midfifties wearing shiny shoes, dress pants with a distinctive crease down the front of each leg, a light blue shirt, and a wide tie. The man handed him an application and showed him to an unoccupied desk to fill it out. The form was very generic, and Zeb had it filled out in no time. He gave the application back to the well-dressed man and was told that if Mercy General was interested in him, they would contact him.

Several weeks went by, and Zeb had heard nothing from Mercy General. He figured his lack of experience probably got his application moved to the bottom of the pile. Then one day, when he got home from work, Janie met him at the front door with a big smile. "Mercy General Hospital called today!" she blurted. "They are offering you the boiler operator position! You have to call them and let them know if you accept it." It was too late to call today, so he would have to call first thing in the morning. He could hardly wait.

The next morning, Zeb called the hospital and got ahold of the switchboard operator who directed his call to the human resources department. The well-dressed man who he had met when filling out the application answered the phone. They discussed a few details, one being that there would be a significant discount on services when Janie has the baby. Zeb's mind was already made up, but the word *discount* clinched it. He accepted the position.

It was now getting close to the end of August. Zeb had worked out a two-week notice at Morton's Garage and the Brice Brother's Grain Mill. He had been at the hospital for a couple of weeks and was totally confused by everything he was trying to learn. He had six months to learn the job before he would be allowed to operate on his own. The operators who were training him reassured him that he was doing fine and that he would learn it all over time.

One morning, while he was packing his lunch, Janie came into the kitchen and told him to pack an extra sandwich. She was going to go to the hospital with him. The baby had decided that it was time to show up.

When they arrived at the hospital, Zeb ran in and got a nurse with a wheelchair to come outside and get Janie. She was whisked up to the maternity ward, and Zeb went to park the car. Before he went to the maternity ward, Zeb went to the boiler room. He flung open the office door and gushed to the operator on duty, "I won't be here today! I will be here, just not down here. I'm having a baby. Well, not me, Janie!" He slammed the door and was gone.

Janie gave birth to an eight-pound ten-ounce redheaded baby girl who they named Rose Elly. Janie and the baby were both fine. Zeb was on another bed in the room, covered in sweat and completely worn out.

2

THE DAYS, WEEKS, AND MONTHS seemed to be flying by. Rose was growing in size and was smart. It was amazing how something so small and young could learn so quickly. Janie was doing wonderful, and she loved everything there was about being a mother. Zeb had completed his training and was on his own in the boiler room. He still had things to learn, but he showed a lot of skill and promise.

Zeb had noticed one thing in the boiler room that puzzled him. Once in a while, he would get the faint smell of pipe tobacco smoke. He recognized the sweet aroma because his grampa Walee had smoked a pipe. He could remember being a small boy sitting on his grandpa's lap watching the smoke drift up in little swirls from the pipe. The smell always gave him a calm, safe, secure feeling.

Zeb had asked the other operators, "Do you smell pipe tobacco smoke in the boiler room?" None of them ever had. He figured it was just a smell he was picking up from something hot, or it was a smell wafting in from outside through the explosion louvers in the walls.

One evening, one of the small pumps that pumped water treatment chemicals into the boilers wasn't pumping. Zeb felt the pump motor, and it was hot. The other operators told him this would occur from time to time, but this was the first time it had happened on his watch.

Common practice was to kill the power, disconnect the piping from the pump, unwire the motor, and replace the whole assembly with a spare from the supply room. He shut off the pump switch, went to the motor control center, and flipped off the breaker, feeding the power to the pump motor. He removed the piping from the pump and was getting ready to unwire the motor when the smell of pipe smoke enveloped him.

He stopped what he was doing and looked around, expecting to see someone smoking a pipe. There was no one there, and there was no visible sign of smoke in the air. He turned back to the task at hand and was about to disconnect the wires from the motor when he heard someone say, "Push the 'start' switch." Zeb stopped what he was doing and just kind of froze in place for a couple of seconds, thinking, *Did I just hear someone?* He started once again to disconnect the motor wires when he heard, even louder than the first time, "Push the 'start' switch."

Zeb spun around really quickly, and there stood a man he had never seen before. The man was small in stature, maybe five feet four inches tall, and a hundred and forty pounds. He was dressed like someone from the early nineteen hundreds. His shoes were brown well-worn dress shoes. He had on dress pants that were perfectly pressed with no wrinkles and had cuffs at the bottom. His shirt was white with small blue stripes, has a high solid white collar, and was buttoned all the way to the top. It looked uncomfortable to him, but the man didn't seem to mind. There was a pair of thin brown suspenders holding up his trousers. The man had thick wavy brown hair, trimmed neatly, and parted on the left. He wore a small pair of round wire glasses, and from the right corner of his mouth rested a pipe with smoke drifting out of it.

Zeb was staring at the man in awe when, once again, he said, "Push the 'Start' switch." Zeb hesitated for a second and then pushed the switch. The motor sparked and began to hum. Zeb went directly to the breaker switch. He had flipped to the off position, but it had not gone all the way to disconnect the power. He flipped the breaker again, making sure this time that the circuit was broken. He then went back to the pump, and the man was gone, and so was the smell of the pipe tobacco smoke.

Zeb didn't know who or what he just saw and experienced. The thought of being electrocuted made him start to shake. Who would take care of Janie and Rose if he was gone? His mind was racing with all kinds of *what-if* questions. Who was this man? Was he a ghost? Was he a guardian angel? Someone who just happened to walk in? How did he know the motor was still energized? Did this really just happen?

3

ZEB NEVER MENTIONED THIS TO Janie because it would only cause her to worry about him being alone at work. He never mentioned it to his coworkers either because they would think he was unstable. He just kept it to himself, and a little part of him hoped he would get the opportunity to meet this man again.

About six months passed, and Zeb had become less obsessed with the man, but the thought of him was still in the back of his mind. While making his routine rounds in the boiler room, it hit him again. The sweet aroma of pipe tobacco smoke. He turned around, and there stood the man again, still dressed in the same clothes as before. Zeb spoke first. "Hello, how are you?"

The man replied, "The same, always the same."

Zeb spoke again. "You left before I had a chance to thank you. Thank you!"

The man smiled, nodded, and puffed on his pipe. "It is not often I get to do that."

"Do what?" Zeb replied.

"Be at a place in time before I have to say, 'Follow this way.'"

Zeb was confused and not sure just what was happening. He did what he thought was right and invited the man into the boiler room office for a chair and a cup of coffee. The man accepted the chair but declined the coffee.

After what seemed like an eternity of silence, although it was only a matter of a few seconds, Zeb began to speak. "Who are you? What are you? Where did you come from?"

The man put his pipe away and started to speak. "My name is Standish. Stan for short. I was once like you. A man who worked every day to support a family, raise my daughter and son right, always follow God's will, and accept it without question. I passed from this world at the age of sixty-eight, which was considered very old at the time."

Zeb blurted out, "So you are a ghost?"

The old man snickered. "Some may say that."

"If you are a ghost, how can I see and talk to you?"

"That's easy," Stan said. "It is God's will."

"What did you mean when you said you have to say, 'Follow this way'?"

"That is very hard to explain, but let me try." So Stan started, "When you pass from this life, that is life in mankind's world, there is more. Eternal life is available after life on earth, just as the Bible says. Jesus Christ did die on the cross so that all sins are forgiven as long as the soul wants them forgiven."

Zeb questioned, "What does that mean?"

"Well, if the soul has repented and believes in Jesus Christ and all of His teachings, he will be accepted into eternal life."

"If not?" Zeb pushed harder, thirsting for answers.

"The soul goes to an empty, lonely place never to be with Jesus and the Father. This is the greatest of all punishments. The soul burns with a desire that will never be fulfilled."

"You still haven't answered my question about 'follow this way,'" Zeb stated.

"When you get eternal life, it is more than the human mind can fathom, so I cannot begin to explain it so that you will understand it." With that, Stan stood up and took a step toward the door and vanished.

Zeb screamed out, "Don't go! Will I see you again?"

Stan's voice replied, "If it is God's will."

Zeb knew he couldn't speak of this encounter, or they would lock him away for being deranged. He did, however, want to learn more, and he knew all the answers were in the Bible.

Zeb and Janie had always been believers in Jesus Christ, and now he wanted to put it into action. They started to attend church on a regular basis, and they took part in Bible study classes. It seemed the more they learned, the more they wanted to learn. Zeb even began to do some volunteer work at the hospital, visiting and praying with patients, whether they were terminally ill or just there for minor ailments. He wanted to bring the Word of God to as many people as possible.

It had been over a year since Zeb's encounter with Standish. He was working the afternoon shift and had just sat down to begin eating his lunch. The familiar smell of pipe tobacco smoke filled his nostrils. He looked up from his bowl of chili, and there sat Standish directly across the office in the same chair that he had been seated before. As always, Zeb spoke first. "Hello, how are you?"

Stan smiled, nodded, and puffed on his pipe. "The same, always the same."

Zeb filled Stan in on all that had happened to him and his family since their last visit. The biggest news was that he and Janie had had another child. They had a little brother for Rose, and they named him James Standish Walee. With that news, Stan smiled and chuckled a little. Zeb told him that it was hard to win Janie over on the name "Standish," but she finally gave in and agreed to it. To this day, the encounters with Stan have been Zeb's only secret from Janie.

"Stan," Zeb asked, "what are you here for? Not just here at Mercy General but back among the living. Are you at other places other than just this hospital?"

Stan sat quietly for a few minutes like he was waiting for permission to speak. Then he started.

"Before I passed from the living, I was very faithful to the teachings of the Bible. Like you, I wanted to know more. I wanted to know just what was expected of me. I tried to live a perfect life as Jesus did, but it was consuming me. The harder I tried, the harder it became. I was distancing myself from family and friends, or I should say, they were distancing themselves from me. All I wanted to talk about was the Bible, Jesus, and how people should be living their lives. One day, it came to me that I can't be perfect. Jesus was and still is the perfect human to walk this earth. I still stayed close to His teachings, but it felt like a great weight was lifted from my shoulders. My family life returned to normal, some friendships were renewed, and some new friendships were made. I found out that you cannot push Jesus on anyone. You can introduce them to each other, but it is up to them to build a relationship."

Zeb sat in dead silence, staring at Stan. What Stan had just revealed to him was the exact path his own life was taking. He himself was consumed with questions and trying to find answers. He was still very close with Janie, Rose, and Jimmy, but there were some friends that he no longer connected with. He should have seen it coming when one coworker told him, "Zeb, you have changed, and it is no fun to even talk with you anymore because I can't live in your 'goody-two-shoes' world."

Zeb finally spoke. "Stan, I have failed, and I think that you somehow already knew that!"

Stan moved his pipe from the right side of his mouth to the left side before he spoke. "Zeb, you have not failed. You are traveling down the right road, but you have drifted toward the berm. Just come back to the center of your lane before you get stuck in the ditch."

Zeb closed his tear-filled eyes. His mind and body felt an overwhelming release of pressure. He questioned Stan, "Where do I go from here?" There was no answer, and when he opened his eyes, Stan was gone.

The rest of his shift was a blur. His mind was racing on what to do next. Forget about all his religious work? Just live and don't worry about sin? Had he put too much pressure on the family? Janie had not complained, but then she never complained about anything, and the kids were still very young. One weight had been lifted from him, but another took its place. "Stan, I wish you would give me the answers!" he yelled at an empty office chair.

5

Zᴇʙ ᴡᴀs sᴛɪʟʟ ᴠᴇʀʏ ᴀᴄᴛɪᴠᴇ in his church, and he still visited with patients regularly. He toned down on expressing his views and pushing the Bible down other people's throats. He gave his thoughts and opinions only when they were asked for. He realized that just being calm, helpful, and polite worked much better at spreading the Word of God rather than giving forced lectures.

Once again, as he was sitting down for his lunch on the afternoon shift, Zeb caught the faint smell of pipe tobacco smoke. The aroma only lasted a few seconds and was gone. Zeb felt a burst of excitement and said, "Stan, are you here?" There was no response from Stan, no tobacco smell from his pipe. The excitement disappeared, and disappointment set in.

The next evening at "lunchtime," Zeb waited with anticipation. Nothing. The next evening was the same—no smoke, no Stan. The following evening, the pipe tobacco aroma came early and caught Zeb by surprise. Stan always showed up on the afternoon or midnight shifts and always at lunchtime.

Stan sat in his usual place, puffing on his pipe. It had been over six years since their first encounter, and not even a hair on Stan's head had changed. Zeb, out of habit, greeted him in the same way. "Hello, how are you?"

The same answer came back from Stan. "Same, always the same."

"I thought you were going to visit a couple of days ago. I thought I smelled the smoke from your pipe," Zeb said with some disappointment in his voice.

"I was here, and I had someone to visit." Stan spoke these words in a low, sad voice.

"So others can see you like I can?" Zeb quipped with excitement in his voice.

"No," Stan replied in a hushed tone. "When others see me, I am there to help them 'follow this way.'"

"So what is it that you do? When someone dies, you are their taxi driver picking them up?" Zeb said this with some agitation in his voice.

"No, it is not like that at all," Stan calmly responded. "I usually arrive sometimes days before their final breath. Some souls do not want to let go of their mortal lives, but their host, or mortal body, in other words, can no longer sustain life. My presence is there to help the soul let go and come 'follow this way.' When there is such love of life and family, the soul hangs on for that love. I am there to help the soul realize there is even greater love, so 'follow this way.'

"When someone is passing, and the only reversal would be the divine intervention of God the Almighty Father, it is wonderful when those around say, 'It is okay to let go.' This somewhat gives the soul permission and a sense of peace. One thing people can do, but usually don't do, is pray for a happy death while they are living. This doesn't mean that death is a party. There still maybe pain or tragedy, but the soul is not afraid, and it is ready to part with the host and 'follow this way.' When the soul parts on its own, I and others like me are not needed. That soul is a believer and will find its way to eternal life with Jesus Christ."

Zeb questioned him further, "You say there are others like you. How many, and why you?"

Stan puffed on his pipe and paused before he spoke. "How many, I do not know, but I do know there are many lost misguided souls that need help. Why me? That's easy. God's will."

"Will you ever get to rest in peace?" Zeb inquired.

"How much more peace can one have than by doing God's will for eternity?" Stan replied.

"It must be very rewarding to collect souls and take them back to heaven," Zeb mentioned.

"There are no rewards, fanfare, or applause. Those are all material things given to living humans. Objects that are always expected just for doing the right things. I was given the opportunity for eternal life at baptism, the greatest gift. It was up to me what to do with that gift. In passing, I was given eternal life with the Father, the Son, and the Holy Ghost. Nothing else now matters or compares. I mentioned to you in the past that you are not capable of understanding what eternal life is. You have to put your faith, hope, love, and trust in Jesus Christ, and 'this way' will come easier for you." With that being said, Stan just disappeared.

"Wait, don't leave yet. I want to know more. I need to know more!" Zeb shouted, but Stan was gone. Zeb sat and thought to himself, *This always happens.* He did a self-examination of his conscience. He and his family wholeheartedly believed in Jesus Christ. Everything that happens is by Jesus's hand, no others. He had a loving wife who was an incredible mother. They, together, have two children who were healthy and smart. Everything they ever needed was provided for them when they needed it. All of this wasn't just luck. There was a higher power in charge.

He wondered if he would be able to do it on his own or if Stan would be there to help him when his time comes to pass on. He began to think of all the people he knew had died. How did it work for them? Was Stan or someone else there to help? Was it easy, or was it difficult? This was too much to think about, and it was kind of disturbing. People have to make their own choices. He just hoped he was making the right ones himself.

6

Days turned into weeks, weeks into months, months into years, and Stan had not been around. Zeb began to wonder if Stan had "moved on" or if he was "busy" doing his work. *Why had Stan appeared to me?* he often pondered. There was nothing special about himself, at least not he was aware of. Why did Stan only show up in the boiler room at Mercy General Hospital and never at home or at church?

Zeb was tiding up the boiler room office, and his mind was wondering aimlessly when he caught the sweet aroma of pipe tobacco smoke. He spun around, and there was Stan, still dressed as he had always been and still looking like the first time Zeb had seen him. "Hello, how are you?" Zeb inquired out of habit.

The reply was predictable, "Same, always the same."

"Well, I am glad you stopped by. I have missed speaking with you," Zeb said with enthusiasm.

"I have been busy," was Stan's answer. "It seems people are moving away from God and His Word, and when their time comes, there is a difficult awakening in which much help is needed. It seems almost everyone gets some religion and calls on the Father and Jesus Christ when their life is not going as they have it planned. A death, an illness, a tragedy, but when their prayers are answered and life turns around for them, the Father and the Son are forgotten until the next time."

Zeb inquired, "What happens to those souls?"

"That I do not know," was Stan's answer. "My job is to help them to understand that it is okay to cross over. Their fate is determined when they stand up for their judgment. In crossing over, I try to help them realize they have to make atonement for the way they lived or didn't live."

"Your job is not an easy one," Zeb said.

"On the contrary, my job is easy. I lay out the truth. It is a simple task because the truth has always been there. There is no way to twist it or disguise it. It is plain and understandable."

"Don't you get frustrated?" Zeb pushed.

"There is no reason to get frustrated. I may be the first exposure to the Word that some souls have ever had, and as you know, touching someone with God's Word is doing God's will."

"Seeing a soul and realizing there is a God would be a joyous occasion," Zeb stated while trying to imagine it.

"I don't see the soul's reaction. I just help them 'follow this way.'

"When someone passes from their human life, they are sometimes confused, scared, or just trying not to go. I and others like me are just there to help. Death is not a frightening experience unless you are totally against the Father and the Son. Jesus died on the cross to forgive all sins, not just the sins of religious souls. Those who do not acknowledge that He exists and that He is the Savior of the world, those are the souls that He will not acknowledge. This, for some, is where it gets scary. Maybe as a child, they were taught about Jesus but lived their life ignoring Him. It is never too late to repent and feel actual sorrow for the sins that have been committed. Actual sorrow is knowing what the sin is and trying to never do it again. This is hard because, at the time of sin, the souls are human. Jesus knows this is difficult because He was human. If repentance and sorrow are there, He will accept the soul. He has told us so many times through His Word. He left His flock of sheep to rescue the one that had wondered. The prodigal son was welcomed home after being away and lost. No matter how many times the soul stumbles and falls, Jesus is there to pick it up and give it another chance. What He wants from the soul is love in return so that the stumbles become fewer and farther between. That love is shown by doing His will and spreading His Word." Stan stopped there and looked at Zeb who was soaking up all that he had said like a sponge.

Zeb found it hard to believe that not everyone believed in Jesus Christ and His teachings. He had always considered the Bible man's owner's manual. He could not imagine life without it.

He looked at Stan and questioned, "What makes people not believe?"

Stan said, "A lot of the time, it is because the Father, the Son, and the Holy Ghost do not fit into their life the way they think they should."

"What do you mean?" Zeb asked.

"Well, when someone prays to God, and they don't get immediate results, they become upset. They fail to realize that God knows what is best, and answering a prayer may do more damage."

"How can an answered prayer do damage?" Zeb was baffled.

"Let me give you a simple example. Say, a prayer is offered up to win the lottery, and the person wins. This will put stress on the winner, will probably cause family and friend fallouts, and possibly destroy their lives. God sees this and does not want this to happen, so the prayer is not answered as requested. Therefore, people get upset with Him. Another example is when they ask for healing, and it doesn't come instantly. Maybe good will come out of the suffering that may stop future suffering for others. Jesus has the ability to heal, but He was sent by the Father to heal souls and to destroy sin and death."

"People still die,' quipped Zeb.

"Those who do not repent die. The others move to 'follow this way' to eternal life."

With that being said, Stan faded away like the wisps of smoke from his pipe. Zeb just sat there with his mind twirling, trying to understand everything he had just heard.

7

YEARS PASSED AS THEY DO, quicker and quicker with each birthday. Zeb was now one of the "old guys" in the boiler room at Mercy General Hospital. Looking back on that first day, he never thought he could learn all there was to know, let alone make it this many years. Zeb had made a good operator, and he had handled many critical situations with a cool mind and a steady hand. He had trained most of the fellows junior to him now. Over time, he had seen many changes from doing almost all operations by hand, to converting 90 percent of the equipment over to the computer age. That in part made him a good operator. He grew right along with the changes, and if circumstances dictated, he could revert to the old ways and run everything manually.

Janie had gone back to teaching after Jimmy started kindergarten many years ago because he was now a freshman in college. She loved helping grow the minds of children, watching them learn, and becoming more independent every day. If teaching five days a week wasn't enough, she also taught Sunday school. She and Zeb believed it was more important to learn the teachings of the Bible, as well as to learn academic lessons. While she taught her class, Zeb and some others took turns teaching adult Bible study. Learning the Word of God doesn't stop when you graduate from school.

One Sunday morning, getting ready to go to church, Zeb heard a thump, and he found Janie unconscious on the bedroom floor. She was still breathing but had a very pale color and was unresponsive. As in the boiler room situation, he stayed very calm. He immediately called 911 for an ambulance and rescue squad. While he waited for them to arrive, he knelt by Janie and prayed harder than he had ever prayed in his life. "Dear Jesus, please lay your healing hands on Janie and let her get up. Lord, I am being selfish in asking, but I can't do it without her. I need her. Rose and Jimmy need her, and she still has more children to teach about You! Please, Jesus, heal her!" By this time, with tears streaming down his face, he could hear the sirens approaching.

Zeb opened the door and let the first responders in and led them to Janie. The EMT knelt next to Janie to assess her, and he looked at his partner with a grim expression and said two words, "Let's hurry!" They placed her on the stretcher and had her loaded into the ambulance in just a matter of minutes and rushed her off to the emergency room of Mercy General Hospital. By the time Zeb arrived, they had already whisked her back to the cardio room. The nursing supervisor caught Zeb at the entrance doors and took him to her office. Zeb was part of the hospital family, so they spared him the experience of sitting in the waiting room. He came to this hospital almost every day, but this was all foreign territory for him—far from the boiler room.

The nursing supervisor helped him call Rose, who was on a retreat weekend for the church. When Rose answered the phone, and Zeb heard her voice, he broke down in tears. The supervisor who knew Rose took the phone. "Rose, this is Kristy Holland at Mercy General Hospital ER. Your mom has suffered a cardiac episode and is still being evaluated by the doctors."

There was silence on the other end.

"Rose, are you still there?"

"Yes, yes, I'm here. I will get someone to drive me, and I will be there in about an hour!"

"Okay, I will let your dad know."

Kristy then phoned Jimmy, who was away at school, and got his voice mail. She left him a message asking him to call her as soon as he could. Kristy was hired into the hospital at the same time that Zeb was, and they went through orientation together. He was in the boiler room, and she was in housekeeping. She had worked at that job while going to nursing school, and occasionally, she would babysit the Walee children for extra money. When she got married and had children of her own, Rose would babysit for her; and when the children were older, they had Janie as a teacher in school. There was a close friendship between these two families.

Her attention turned back to Zeb, who had regained his composure and was now sitting by the window. He had a small well-worn Bible in his hand, and he was reading to himself. Reassuringly, she touched him on the shoulder and told him the kids were on their way. She reminded him that Janie was a strong woman and that everything would be okay.

After about half an hour, the doctor on duty came into the office. "Mr. Walee," he said to Zeb, "your wife has suffered a major cardiac event."

"Will she be okay?" Zeb demanded to know.

"I will be honest with you," replied the doctor. "I am not sure at this time, but she is still alive and stable, which is a good sign. I have put a call to the cardio specialist, Dr. Amal, and I am waiting for his return call. The next few hours will be critical, but I am optimistic, and I need you to be also."

"Can I be with her?" he asked.

"For a few minutes, but I have to warn you. There are a lot of tubes and monitors—"

Before he could finish, Zeb interrupted, "That's okay. I want to be with her!"

The doctor took Zeb back and said, "You can only stay for a few minutes, and then we are moving her to the cardiac care unit where Dr. Amal will be able to evaluate her further when he arrives."

Zeb took Janie's hand in his and squeezed it. She had better color than she did at the house. He bent over and kissed her on the forehead and squeezed her hand again. He whispered, "There is strength in these hands together. Let them not be separated." He then prayed out loud. "Lord Jesus, we have always tried to live by Your Word and do Your will. Please, Lord, hear my prayer to heal Janie and make her strong."

They moved her to the critical care unit, and Zeb went to the waiting room to pray and just wait. Rose arrived and prayed and cried with her dad. She could not imagine life without her mom. Jimmy had called her after getting the message from Kristy, and she filled him in on their mother's condition. He was on his way, but it would still be a while before he could get there.

Several of their church family had shown up at the hospital to offer comfort, but they were not allowed in the unit, so Rose went downstairs to meet with them. No way was Zeb leaving that floor, just not yet. Someone somehow at the church had gotten word on what had happened. After the Sunday service, no one left the church for another hour or so. They continued to pray and sing hymns.

It had been several hours since Janie had had her *event*. The cardio specialist had arrived and was running a multitude of tests on her, so they were being told by the nurses. Finally, Dr. Amal came into the room to speak with Zeb, Rose, and Jimmy who had just arrived. "Mrs. Walee," he said.

"Her name is Janie!" Zeb snapped back.

Rose put her arm around him to ease him. "Janie," Dr. Amal started over, "is in very critical condition, but she is stable. From a medical standpoint, that is very encouraging, but there are no promises because we are not sure yet what has caused this problem. We are still waiting on the results of several tests and images to come back, but let me assure you that we are doing everything we can at this time. And if there is any change at all, we will let you know." Having said that, the doctor turned and left the room.

They sat quietly for a while, and Zeb got up and said, "I am going down to the boiler room for a bit." Jimmy wanted to go with him, but Zeb wanted to go alone. He reminded them of the phone extension there and said to have the nurse call if there was any change.

ZEB WENT TO THE BOILER room office and met the operator on shift and told him a little about what was going on. He asked him if he would go make rounds and leave him in the office alone for a while. He wanted to be someplace familiar and comfortable to let his mind settle. The operator obliged and left.

Once he was alone, Zeb called out, "Stan are you here? Show up!" Nothing. After a few minutes, he tried again. "Stan, I know you hear me. Show up!" Still nothing. After about an hour of calling out and Stan not showing up, the operator returned. Zeb thanked him and told him to pass it on that he was taking time off until things changed one way or another. The operator said that he would and that they would all be praying for Janie's recovery.

It was now Tuesday morning, and there still had been no change, and the doctors were still running tests, trying to figure out what was going on. Zeb had only left the hospital to go home to shower and change clothes. In the last forty-eight hours, he had eaten very little and had almost no sleep. Rose and Jimmy had tried to get him away, but he would not leave for fear of losing Janie while he was gone. He had even gotten a little mean with them by snapping at them when they suggested he sleep or eat. He had never been cross with his kids, even when disciplining them; he always spoke calmly. They understood his actions because they knew he was exhausted and worried.

He went to the hospital chapel to pray, but once there, he turned all of his anger on the Lord. "You know, Lord," he started, "all of our lives, Janie and I have been devoted to You, believed in

You, and trusted in You. And now we really need You, and you have abandoned us. Stan is not around either. Maybe he was just a figment of my imagination. Maybe all the time spent in church and sharing Your Word was a wasted time. Maybe You DON'T exist!" With that said, Zeb just sat there for a short time until he felt a hand on his shoulder, and he heard Rose's voice. "Dad, the doctor wants to meet with us downstairs in his office."

They met Jimmy at the doctor's office and went in. Dr. Shilo Amal looked much different from when they saw him in the waiting room with his scrubs on. He was a small man with jet-black hair and deep-brown skin, and for some reason, which they had not noticed before, he had a slight southern accent. After inviting them all to sit down, he rolled his chair up to his desk, leaned forward, and folded his hands on top of some paperwork in front of him.

"After examining Janie"—he looked directly at Zeb for some reaction—"we have found a small growth in her main heart artery. It is not a blood clot, which is what usually causes a heart attack and is sometimes fatal. This growth is allowing enough blood flow to pass, allowing her to stay alive. We have found no evidence of any heart damage or brain damage at this time."

"Then why isn't she awake?" Zeb demanded.

"Like I stated," Dr. Amal continued, "there is still blood flowing, but her body has shut down to protect itself because of the diminished flow."

Jimmy spoke for them all. "Okay, Doc, what is the next step? Can you remove this growth?"

"I believe we can, my team and me. However, with any surgery, there are risks involved and no guarantees."

"What if you don't do surgery? Can you dissolve it?" Rose questioned.

"Unfortunately, surgery is the only option, and without it, nothing will change, and her body will start to give away. However, I need your permission to perform the surgery."

"There is no question on what has to be done," stated Zeb in a week voice. "When will you do it?"

"I will call and have an OR readied right now, and I will call in my handpicked team," replied the doctor.

"Can we be with her before you take her to surgery?" Rose asked, fighting back tears.

"Yes, go straight up to the unit, and I will have them let you back in with her until we are ready, which should be in about an hour."

They stood up and shook hands with Dr. Amal and thanked him. When they turned to leave, Zeb noticed a tobacco pipe on the shelf that resembled the one that Stan smokes. Zeb turned back to the doctor and said to him, "I am surprised that a heart surgeon would smoke a pipe."

Dr. Amal replied, "I don't smoke. I am not sure where that came from. Maybe one of the cleaning people left it there." Having heard this, there was no explanation for the pipe being there. It gave Zeb a little sense of comfort that maybe Stan was around, and at the same time, it gave him a sense of anger.

THEY WENT UP TO THE critical care unit to sit with Janie until it was time for her surgery. The nurse on duty met them at the elevator and escorted them back to her room. "Doctor Amal said the OR would be ready in about an hour, and I will come and get you when it is time to go," she said in an almost whisper of a voice.

Janie looked as though she was sleeping. Her color was good, but her hair was a mess. It was a good thing she was asleep because being around people with messed-up hair would have embarrassed her to no end. To all three of them, though, she was beautiful.

Zeb went to one side of the bed and took her hand in his. He had to hold back the tears so he would look strong for the kids. Rose went to the other side of the bed and held her mother's other hand. Jimmy stood at the foot of the bed. He didn't say a word, but tears slowly rolled down his cheeks and dripped from his jaw.

Zeb started to speak. "Janie, I don't know if you can hear me or not. The doctor tells us that you have a small growth in your heart that is not letting enough blood get through. They are going to take you to surgery and remove it. After they are finished, you will be as good as new, and we can all go home. When you wake up, I bet you will be starved. All you have had for the last few days is IV fluids. When you get back on your feet, we will all go to that barbeque buffet place that you like so much. How does that sound? Like a plan?"

Rose chimed in, "Yeah, and we will tell them that it is Jimmy's birthday, so they will sing 'Happy Birthday to You' to him, and we can watch his face turn red!" The three of them chuckled. It was the first time any of them had smiled in several days.

They continued to make small talk, including her in the conversation even though there was no response. Thy told her that the church family had met several times to offer prayers and sing hymns for her recovery. They told her that so much food had been brought to the house that they no longer have any place to put them, so their next-door neighbor had been bringing it to the hospital to feed the staff.

There was a light tap at the door, and then it cracked open slowly. It was the nurse with the whispered voice and two other staff members. "They are ready for her in the OR now," she whispered softly. "So we have to get her ready."

Zeb bent down and kissed Janie on the cheek and said, "I love you!" Rose squeezed her mom's hand and said, "It is all going to be okay!" Jimmy squeezed passed his sister and leaned over and kissed his mom on the forehead. When he did this, he started to sob. Rose put her arm around him, and they left the room—the three of them all together. The nurse instructed them where to go so that when the surgery was over, Dr. Amal would know where to find them.

Rose looked at her dad and Jimmy and said, "The surgery will take some time, so let's go to the chapel for a little while."

Her dad hesitated before he spoke. "You to go ahead. Maybe I will join you later."

This seemed a bit odd to the kids because they knew of no one with stronger faith than their dad, but the last few days had not been in any way normal.

As the kids went to the chapel, Zeb made his way to the boiler room. He went into the office, only to find it empty. The operator must have been making his rounds or handling a call in the hospital somewhere. He sat down at the desk and took a couple of deep breaths, hoping to catch the smell of pipe tobacco smoke. Nothing. He once again tried calling out to Stan, but again, there was no response. The boiler operator came in, and they talked for a few minutes, and Zeb filled him in on Janie's condition. Zeb excused himself to go to the surgical waiting room and do just that, wait.

10

ZEB ARRIVED AT THE WAITING room, a large room, and he looked around to find Rose and Jimmy, but they were not there yet. There were, however, four other groups, families, huddled in little clusters throughout the room. He looked at each group, trying to imagine why they were here.

The first group was a man and a woman who looked to be in their late twenties. With them was a little girl about four years old with brown curly hair and an endless array of questions. There was also an older couple, probably a set of grandparents. All attention was on the little girl trying to keep her quiet and entertained.

The next group was of three men and three women, all middle-aged. The way they were sitting, he concluded they were married couples. The two men and one woman must have been siblings because they resembled one another a great deal. They were not speaking much, and all six of them had the look of worry and sadness on their faces.

The third group was an elderly man who looked to be in his eighties, and he was in a wheelchair. Along with him was a man and a woman, late middle-aged. They could have been his children or one child and a spouse. They spoke loudly so that the elderly gentleman could hear them. They called him "Dad," and they reassured him the mom was going to be okay, but he just sat there and cried. Zeb thought this was almost a mirror image of him and the kids.

The last group seemed upbeat. There were seven of them in all, looking to be in their twenties. They had several conversations going on, but they were not disrupting anyone.

Rose and Jimmy came in and sat next to him. They had stopped at the cafeteria and got something to drink. They brought him a cup of coffee and a couple of chocolate chip cookies. To their amazement, he accepted both. He even commented that the cookies were almost as good as their mom's.

After some quiet time together, Rose gave in and asked, "Dad, what's bothering you? We know Mom is on your mind. She is on all of our minds. You seem to have an anger that we have never seen before, and that scares us too."

Zeb sat quietly for a few moments, and then he looked at Rose and spoke. "Rose, honey, all of my life, I have tried to live by God's Word, do His will, and spread His teachings. I like to think that your mother and I have taught you kids to love God with your whole heart, mind, soul, and body and to put Him first before all others. Now when I need Him most, He is not there for me, for us. Why is your mother going through this? Why are we going through this? What did we do wrong to deserve this?" Then Zeb began to sob. He was as low as he had ever been in his life. Not only could he be losing his wife, but his God had also forsaken him, not heard him, not come to his rescue. His anger was brought on by his sadness and a sense of mourning.

Rose and Jimmy just sat there with their minds swirling. The strongest, most faithful man they knew was sitting in front of them beaten down. They didn't know what to say, but they both knew what to do. Both, silently, prayed for strength and guidance for themselves, for their father, and for their mother.

After a while, Rose began to try and comfort her dad. "You know, Dad, I don't know why this happened, but God has been here with you from the start. I think maybe you were too shocked and scared to realize it. He made sure you were home with Mom when this happened and not alone. He made sure the ambulance got her here quickly. He made sure that this hospital has a heart specialist on staff and that he was available. He let it happen on a Sunday when the church family was all together to offer prayers. Most of all, He has kept her alive and safe for us. He has not abandoned you. He has stood with you strongly, handling everything while you were overcome with fright. Why He let it happen, I don't know, but He knows we trust Him, and in time, we will accept His will. He loves us more than we can ever return to Him."

Zeb looked at her with a sense of calm. "Out of the mouths of babes," he said, and they all put their arms around each other and hugged.

Their wait seemed like an eternity, but it had actually only been a little over ninety minutes. The doctor had not given them any indication of how long the surgery would take. All they could do was wait and try to keep their minds occupied with their surroundings.

11

A DOCTOR APPEARED AT THE door in the hallway coming from the operating rooms. When he took his mask down, they realized that it was not Dr. Amal. The doctor looked around the room and spotted the family with the little brown-haired girl, and he walked over to them.

When he reached them, the little girl, whose name they now learned as Priscilla, gave him a thorough interrogation. "Are you the doctor that pulled out my brother's tonsils?" she questioned. Her parents tried to pull her back and hush her, but the doctor motioned to let her talk.

"Yes, I am, and he is doing wonderful," the doctor answered.

Priscilla continued, "Are you going to put them back after you make them better?"

"No, by the time they get better, your brother will have outgrown them." The doctor seemed to be enjoying this conversation.

"Are you going to have to take my tonsils out too?" she questioned.

"I don't know. Let me see. Open your mouth real wide, and I will check them out." By this time, the whole room was paying attention to what was going on. "Your tonsils look just fine, so I think you can keep them!"

"That's good because I don't want to give them away."

The doctor patted her on the head, and she turned away, so he now focused on the parents. "Your son should be in recovery for about an hour, and then you can take him home. The recovery nurse will give you a list of instructions to follow for the next several days. Does anyone have any questions?" He turned and looked at Priscilla, but she was busying doing something else and had lost interest in him.

Just then, another surgeon came out, and they knew right away it was not Dr. Amal. This doctor was a thirty-something young lady. She made her way over to the group of young people. Evidently, one of their friends was showing off on the backyard trampoline and landed on the cement sidewalk, breaking his ankle. The doctor assured the group that everything went okay, but their friend would probably be staying in the hospital for a few days. They were all high-fiving, hugging, and laughing. Zeb felt happy for them, but his own anxiety was starting to build. How much longer was it going to be before Dr. Amal would come out?

A little while later, a third surgeon appeared from the operating room area. He, too, was not Dr. Amal. This man was middle-aged, well over six feet tall, and very athletic looking. He stopped at the edge of the room and announced, "Barthow family?" The couple with the elderly gentleman in the wheelchair raised their hand, and the doctor made his way over to them. He spoke in a loud voice that the father would not be excluded from the conversation. "Mrs. Barthow is doing well. Her hip replacement was a textbook case. Her vital signs are strong. There was minimal blood loss, and she should make a full recovery. We are going to keep her for a few days and do some physical therapy with her, and then she will be able to go home." The elderly gentleman had tears streaming down his face, but he was smiling as he reached out to shake the doctor's hand and thank him. The doctor took the gentleman's hand in both of his and spoke directly to him. "The nurse will come and get you when they take her up to her room, and then you can go be with her." The doctor shook hands with the man and woman as they thanked him, and then he returned in the direction that he came.

Still no word on Janie. Could something have gone wrong? Were they having trouble with the surgery? Surely, if it was something bad, they would have heard something. The waiting was getting to be stressful. Jimmy spoke. "Dad, I am going to go get something to drink. Why don't you come with me?"

"Yeah, Dad, go stretch your legs. You won't be gone that long. The cafeteria is just down the hall. Besides, I am here, and if the doctor comes out, I will call Jimmy." Rose had inherited her dad's ability to stay calm, and it had revealed itself through this whole ordeal.

A few minutes after they had left, another surgeon came out; but again, it was not the doctor they had been waiting on. This fellow was small in stature like Dr. Amal, but he was much older. He walked slowly over to the three couples who had been waiting almost in silence the whole time. He spoke softly, but with no other noise in the room, Rose couldn't help but overhear. "I removed a mass from your brother's right kidney"—the doctor hesitated to compose his words—"but the cancer has spread to all of his major organs. There was no way that I could get it all."

The group held on to one another a little tighter, and some started to cry. "What now, Doctor?" asked one of the men.

"Well, we can start treatments that may help prolong life for several more weeks, or we can just let the cancer take its course. When your brother wakes up from recovery, we will move him up to a room. I will let him sleep tonight, and then tomorrow, I will explain the options to him. I would like for a couple of you, the fellows, to be there if possible. Sometimes, the news is easier to take if there are no women present. I hope you understand." They shook their heads, and the doctor said, "I am sorry." He turned and walked away, and the family slowly left. Rose thought to herself, *God is still taking care of us.* He got her dad out of the room so that he didn't have to experience that.

Zeb and Jimmy came back and looked around the waiting room. It was empty except for Rose. Jimmy handed her a coffee and said, "I bet the next doctor through the door will be Dr. Amal." Just then, the door opened, and Dr. Amal came through it and walked directly over to them. "Everything went well," he said. "I removed the blockage from her heart, and her blood pressure went back to normal. It was a small muscle growth that resembled the uvula in the back of your throat. It could have been there all of her life, and it just happened to move in such a way that it got stuck this time. It was sent out to pathology, which is the standard procedure."

"When can we see her?" Zeb questioned.

"She is in recovery now, and I want to keep her sedated overnight. How about we say late morning tomorrow? Why don't you guys go have a nice dinner and get a good night's sleep. I am sure you can use it. She is going to be okay now."

"Thank you, Doctor," said Rose as she gave him a hug.

"When will she be able to go home?" Jimmy wanted to know.

"Probably the day after tomorrow or the next day for sure," replied Dr. Amal with a big smile. "Now go on, you guys. Get out of here. I have patients to check on. I will see or talk with you tomorrow."

12

THEY LEFT THE HOSPITAL THAT night and went home to have supper. It felt like they had been away for months. There were tons of food in the refrigerator that had been brought by friends, neighbors, and members of their church family. They pulled out dishes and bowls, and they each fixed a plate. They sat at the kitchen table, talked, and laughed. This was something they hadn't done for several days, and it felt like a huge weight had been lifted off of their shoulders. Maybe things were starting to get back to some sense of normalcy.

After the kitchen had been cleaned up, they all turned in for the night. Zeb woke up at 4:00 a.m., which was not unusual for him. He went out on the back porch and sat on the swing where he and Janie had spent a lot of mornings watching the sun rise and a lot of evenings watching the sun set. He sat there in the dark, listening to the quiet. His mind was not focused on anything but the quiet. As the sun began to creep up, he started to reflect on the past several days. Not about Janie, but about himself.

Zeb started to speak out loud. "Lord God, Almighty Father, forgive me. How quickly I lost my faith and trust in You when things didn't go my way. At a time when You had complete control as always, I doubted You, I was angry with You, and I wandered from You. My heart and soul ache because I betrayed You. Still, You showed Your love for me by taking care of us in Your own way and time. Father, please forgive me and show mercy to me, for I am truly sorrowful for what I have done." Zeb broke down and started to weep.

It was about 6:00 a.m. when Rose came out on to the porch. "I knew I would find you here," she said.

Zeb had collected himself by now, and he answered her. "I never miss a chance to be out here and watch the sun rise. What are you doing up so early?"

"I never want to miss a chance to see the sun rise," was her quick response. They sat on the swing together, quietly watching the light from the sun spread across the land, and they could feel the warmth beginning to rise.

After about an hour, they went inside, made a pot of coffee, and sat at the kitchen table. Jimmy appeared, got a fork out of the silverware drawer, and began eating a chocolate cake that was sitting on the countertop. "Nutritious breakfast?" his sister questioned.

"I think so," came his quick reply.

"Well, bring it over here and share it!" she responded.

Zeb liked having them both home again. "When are we going to go get Mom?" Jimmy wanted to know.

"I think we will go to the hospital around eleven. That gives us all time to shower and get ready. Don't get your hopes up. I don't think they will release her for a day or two," was Zeb's reply.

They got ready and left the house, and when they got to the hospital, they didn't have any idea where to look for her. Rose walked up to the information desk in the lobby and asked the lady seated there, "Can you tell me what room Mrs. Jane Walee is in?"

"Room 422. Your dad will know how to get there, so I don't have to explain it to you," she answered with a smile. Zeb thanked her, and they went to the elevator to go to the fourth floor.

When they got off the elevator, they looked at the room numbers on the wall. Room 422 was to the right all the way to the end of the hall. As they approached the room, they could hear a man laughing. When they walked in, there was Dr. Amal, who seemed very upbeat. "Well, the gangs are all here!" the doctor said. "She is doing very well. I explained to her what had happened and what has taken place the last several days. I see no sign of any issues other than she is still a bit groggy. I think she will be able to go home tomorrow with some restrictions. We will talk more about that when she is released.

Right now, I think you guys need to visit, but she needs rest, so don't stay all day!" Having said that, he waved and left the room. You could still hear him speaking to everybody all the way to the elevators.

Janie was sitting up in bed, and her color was much better than it had been. Zeb and both kids gave her a hug and a kiss. She looked at them and said, "I am so sorry for what I have put you through. I am sure you were scared, but there was no need to be. God has this. He is in charge. When the time does come for me to pass on many, many years from now, don't be scared or sad. I will be with Jesus for eternity. It is what I have worked for all of my life." After pausing, Janie blurted out, "I must look a mess. My hair feels matted. Rose, do you have a brush in your purse?"

Zeb interrupted, "Janie, you look beautiful. Your voice is beautiful, and your spirit is beautiful!"

They stayed with her most of the afternoon. Rose got the hairbrush she brought from home because she knew her mother would be worried about how she looked, so she brushed her mother's hair for her and fixed it the best she could. Zeb helped her with her lunch tray, and he apologized for the hospital food. "Now you know why I always bring your cooking to work with me."

Jimmy told his mom, "I'm sorry that you didn't get any of the chocolate cake that Mrs. Markson brought over."

Rose gave him a stern look and said, "Wait a minute. There was still half a cake on the table when we left home!"

"I know," said Jimmy, "but I haven't had lunch or supper yet!"

"Okay, okay, you two." Zeb stepped in. "It is time for us to go. Your mom needs her rest." Zeb looked back at Janie and said, "In some ways, they are still little kids, but in others, they are very mature adults. We will be back tomorrow to take you home with us. Get some rest. We love you very much." With that, they left so that she could get some sleep.

13

THE NEXT MORNING, ZEB'S PHONE rang, and he answered it. "Zeb?" came the voice on the other end. "This is Samantha Trent, the charge nurse on level four."

Zeb's heart sank. "Is something wrong with my wife?" he choked out.

"No, no, no, I am so sorry if I scared you. She wants you to bring her hairbrush when you come to pick her up today. She said she is not leaving until she fixes her hair! Also, she wants her white tennis shoes, blue slacks, and a matching top. She said for Rose to pick out the top, not you! Have you got all that?"

"Yes, Samantha, I do. Hairbrush, white tennis shoes, blue slacks, and matching top." After he hung up, he smiled to himself. He was getting his Janie back.

Zeb and the kids arrived at the hospital and went to the fourth level. When they got off the elevator, Samantha looked up from the nurse's station and said, "Rose, did you pick out the top?"

"Yes," she answered with a big smile.

They went into Janie's room, and she was sitting on the edge of the bed, waiting for them. Nobody would ever guess that she had had heart surgery a few days ago. A nurse, who looked to be about seventeen years old, followed them into the room. "I'm nurse Shelly Stoker, and I have a list of 'rules' that Mrs. Walee must follow!" She may have looked seventeen, but she had the confidence and authoritative voice of a forty-year-old drill sergeant! They all stopped what they were doing to pay strict attention to her for fear that they would

38

get scolded if they didn't! When she finished, she handed Zeb an appointment card for Dr. Amal's office one week from today. "If there are no questions, Mrs. Walee, I wish you a speedy recovery." No one said a word, and she turned and left the room. At one time, they all let out a sigh of relief.

Rose helped her mother do her hair and get dressed. They went through all the formalities of being discharged, and when she got outside, she was happy with the smell of fresh air and the warmth of the sun. On the ride home, she was noticing things that she hadn't seen before or just had not noticed. The colors seemed to be more vibrant. The sounds of little things, like the birds singing, seemed to push their way to the front of her conscience. She was beginning to realize how close she must have been to passing away.

They pulled into the driveway, and when they got out of the car, Rose and Jimmy took their mother's things into the house. Zeb went around to help Janie get out of the car, and when she stood up, he stopped her. He looked deep into her eyes and said, "I need you to do me two favors. First, follow all of these 'rules' no matter how well you feel. I don't want any complications because I can't go through this again. Second, don't ever leave me!"

She looked back at him with strong love. "I will follow all the 'rules' for you and for the kids. I am sorry for having to put you all through this. As for the second favor, I have no intention of leaving you, but we both know we are not in control of that. When one of us does pass on, God will be there to comfort the other, and the one still here should not be sad but happy because the other is in Jesus's arms."

Zeb kissed her and led her into their home, hand in hand.

Janie stayed true to her promise and followed all the 'rules.' At her follow-up appointment with Dr. Amal a week later, some of the 'rules' were dropped. He did, however, remind her that she had just had major surgery and that she still had to progress slowly on her way to a full recovery. It would be six months before all 'rules' would be lifted, and she could go back to a complete life of normalcy.

The following week, Zeb would be returning to work on the night shift, which worked out in his favor. Rose would be home at night, and he would be home in the daytime. He trusted Janie's word on doing his favors, but a little assurance never hurt. God makes all things work out!

14

Zeb returned to work, and life was getting back to normal. He liked the viewpoint of the hospital better from the boiler room rather than the viewpoint he had a couple of weeks ago. There would be days at a time when he never left the boiler area, and it seemed that doctors, nurses, and patients were people he seldom heard about. He liked it that way.

On his third night back, he was just finishing his lunch when he smelled pipe tobacco smoke. He looked across the room, and Stan was sitting in the same chair he always sat in. Zeb was hesitant for a moment because he didn't know what emotion was going to come out—happiness for seeing Stan or anger for Stan not being there when he needed him.

"Hello," said Zeb.

Stan puffed on his pipe and nodded.

"How are you?" Zeb asked with some stiffness in his voice.

"Same, always the same," came Stan's usual reply.

Zeb could hold back no longer, "Where were you when I needed you?"

"I go where God sends me, where I am needed. I was not needed here," Stan said very calmly.

"I needed you!" Zeb shot back.

"Were you in need of help to 'follow this way'?" Stan questioned.

"Well, no," muttered Zeb.

"Then you didn't need me," Stan replied.

"Janie was in a bad way. I almost lost her."

"Did Janie need help to 'follow this way'?" Stan questioned.

"No, I don't think so. I don't know. I can't speak for others." Zeb was starting to get frustrated.

"When you are in trouble," Stan explained, "you need to seek Jesus's help through prayer. I and the others like me cannot help. You can ask Jesus's mother, Mary, to intercede for you with her Son. You can ask the saints to pray to Jesus on your behalf. Did you do that?"

"Yes, yes, I did," replied Zeb, "but no one heard my prayers. I was left all alone."

There was silence between the two for several minutes, and Stan began to speak. "You once asked me, 'What makes people not believe in Jesus Christ and His teachings?' Are you a true believer in Jesus Christ, Zeb?"

"You know that I am!" Zeb fired back.

"When you thought you were losing Janie, did your faith quickly turn anger in which you thought maybe it was all false and that you wasted your time worshiping God?"

"Yes," Zeb replied in a low, sorrowful voice.

"You didn't get what you wanted in an instant, and fear took over. Your faith was tested, and you failed, but you are human, and God knows this. Jesus fell three times on the way to Calvary because he was human. God was not angry with you. Saddened, yes, but not angry. He did not abandon you. He was there in every way, from the quick ambulance crew to the hospital staff to the skill in the hands of the surgeon. He had control you didn't. You thought you were alone, and that scared you. You were never alone."

"I am so sorry," Zeb said through tears.

"That is a sign of a true believer," Stan comforted. "You are truly sorry, and faced with the same situation again, your faith will be tested again, and maybe the anger will come again but maybe slower. Always remember, it is God's will to be done, not yours. Pray for the ability to accept it, not to try and change it."

"I will try," said Zeb. "I will surely try. I have always considered myself a deeply religious person, and I slipped. I can't imagine how hard your job must be to convince those who do not know Jesus Christ to 'follow this way.'"

"It is not a hard job at all. I just do God's will as He instructs me. If everyone would do this, their lives and the whole world would be so much better. He has all the right answers, and He has given them out, but humans think they know better than Him."

"I would like to know more about what you do and how you do it if that is allowed?" Zeb asked again.

"Maybe some time. It is His will." With that being said, Stan faded away. Zeb sat and thought about all they had talked about, and then he bowed his head. "Lord Jesus, I thank You for all that You do for us, and I am sorry for having let my faith fail. Your will be done, and help me to accept it."

15

MONTHS PASSED, AND LIFE RETURNED to normal. Janie had completely recovered, and she felt better than she ever had. She was back to her teaching job with new energy and a strong passion. Rose was still trying to choose her life's direction, but she was happy. Jimmy was away at college, enjoying life to the fullest. Both still held strong to their faith and beliefs, probably which explains their happiness.

Zeb was still working in the boiler room at Mercy General Hospital, looking at a few more years before retirement. He had not talked to Stan in a while, and he never knew if he would talk to him again. After all of these years, he never mentioned Stan to anyone, not even to Janie. It always puzzled him why God picked him for Stan to appear to, but as Stan says, it is God's will.

At around two in the morning, on night shift, Zeb smelled the pipe tobacco smoke, and there was Stan. "Hello, how are you?" Zeb said with a grin because he knew what the reply would be.

"Same, always the same." After he said that, Stan disappeared, and the aroma of the pipe smoke was gone. Zeb was sad because he enjoyed his talks with his friend, and this was unusual for him to show up and just leave again.

After a few minutes of Stan not returning, Zeb stepped outside to get some fresh air. He could hear a siren coming, but this was not unusual; after all, this was a hospital. As the siren got closer, he could tell there was more than one. Out of curiosity, he walked up around the corner of the building to where the ER entrance was. Two ambulances rolled in, and before they could off-load, a third came in with a siren and lights. He stood at a distance and watched. A bright light in the sky at a distance caught his eye. As the light got closer, he could hear the blades of a helicopter, and he knew it was coming there. As he watched the medical helicopter land, a fourth ambulance rolled in. He thought to himself, *The ER staff is sure busy tonight.* He turned to walk to the boiler room when he saw another bright light in the sky appear. He waited to see where it would land because the first one was on the helipad. It was then that he noticed a fifth ambulance pulling up to the ER doors. *This can't be good*, he thought. Looking back at the second helicopter, he watched it land in the staff parking lot. Since it was the off shift, there were only a few cars there, so the pilot had plenty of room to sit down. Zeb made it back to the boiler room, and luckily, his night was a routine with no excitement.

Around 5:00 a.m., Hershel, the midnight security guard, stopped in the boiler room office for a cup of coffee. Hershel was seventy-one years old but was still in excellent condition. He was six feet six inches tall and weighed about two hundred forty pounds. If a physical situation got out of hand, you would want Hershel on your side! "The ER had a bad scene tonight," he said, making conversation.

"Yeah, I saw all the activity at once up there. I wondered where they were going to put that second helicopter," Zeb responded.

"Yeah, a drunk driver crossed the yellow line and hit a family in a small car."

"How bad?" Zeb questioned.

"The drunk was DOA. Thirty-year-old mother and four-year-old son died shortly after arrival. The father and the two-year-old daughter were flown out."

"May God have mercy on their souls and may He heal the survivors," Zeb said out loud.

"Amen," said Hershel. "Amen. Thanks for the coffee. See you tomorrow."

"Yep, see you tomorrow, Hershel."

When Zeb got home that morning, the wreck was on the news. The names had not been released, but they did say that the father and daughter had been flown to the University Trauma Hospital which was about hundred and fifty miles north of Leets. No information was available on their conditions. When Janie came into the living room, Zeb explained to her what had happened. They prayed together for the victims, their families, and those who are usually forgotten about—the first responders and ER staff.

Janie finished getting ready to head out to school, and Zeb took a shower to try and wind down so he could go to bed and sleep. While lying in bed, his thoughts turned to Stan. Could the accident have had something to do with his leaving so quickly?

16

Zᴇʙ ᴡᴀs ʙᴀᴄᴋ ᴀᴛ ᴡᴏʀᴋ the next night when the familiar aroma of pipe smoke caught his nose. He looked up, and there was Stan. Instead of the usual greeting, Zeb said, "I didn't expect to see you again so soon."

"I was needed elsewhere when I last visited," Stan said.

"Did it have anything to do with the bad car accident?" questioned Zeb.

There was no response from Stan.

"How do you know when and where to go?" Zeb pushed for some type of answer.

"He knows where I am needed, and I follow His will."

"He referring to God?" replied Zeb.

"Yes, there is no other will to follow than that of the Almighty Father."

Zeb again inquired, "Were you needed at the wreck?"

There was a pause like Stan was waiting for permission to speak. "Yes."

After a few more minutes of silence, Zeb spoke. "I would imagine it was hard for the driver to cross over after what he had just done."

Again, Stan looked like he was waiting for permission to speak. "It was not the driver. It was the child." They both sat in silence for what seemed like an eternity, Stan not saying anything and Zeb not knowing what to say.

"Why would an innocent child have trouble going straight to heaven?" Zeb said, finally breaking the silence.

Stan began to speak freely. "The child's soul was scared. It was not a matter of sorrow for sin or not. It was confused. It didn't want to leave the child. It did not yet have an understanding of life and death. Everything that it did know had just been taken away. There was no one to guide it."

"So that is where you come in?" Zeb asked.

"Yes, I am there to comfort the soul and to let it know it is okay. Once I get it on the path to 'follow this way,' everything is calm and beautiful. When I hear a child's soul shout with excitement, 'Mommy,' I know they have entered the arms of the Blessed Virgin Mary. She also greets all the aborted souls and gives them the love they were denied."

"What about the other two souls that perished in the accident?" Zeb wanted to know.

"I know nothing of them, only the one that the Father willed me to help," was Stan's response.

Once again, silence filled the room. "I want to know because I am curious. Why are you telling me now when you would not tell me before what you do?" asked Zeb.

"I only tell what the Father wants me to tell. Maybe there is a message for you in what I speak of. That is something you will have to figure out or something you will never figure out. Remember, I have told you that the human mind cannot grasp all. Do not be over-whelmed by what you have heard. There is a purpose, but it will be revealed in His time, not yours. Patience." With that, Stan was gone.

Zeb thought about what was said all night and for the next several days. He tried not to get bogged down by it, but that was hard. Talking with Stan was like being one step away from God Himself. Then he thought, *I talk with God myself daily without a third party.* Why was Stan sent to him? What is he supposed to do with what he has learned? Stan was right; this was all too much for him to understand. The only thing he could do was pray for courage, knowledge, and understanding to accept God's will.

17

OVER A YEAR HAD PASSED since Stan had last visited Zeb. Zeb had not forgotten about him, but it had been a while since he had thought about him. He was still very true to his faith, but he had stopped trying to figure out God's plan for him. He knew everything that happens is God's will, and so far, it all has been going pretty well for him.

One evening, while sitting in the boiler room office, there it was—the sweet smell of pipe tobacco smoke. When he looked up, there was Stan, sitting in his usual chair. Nothing about Stan ever changed. He looked exactly the same now as he did those many years ago when he kept a young boiler operator from being electrocuted.

"Hello, how are you?" Zeb asked, and he waited on the reply.

"Same, always the same."

"I haven't seen you in a while. I hope you haven't been busy."

"It gets busier every day," was Stan's answer. "More and more people are moving away from the Father, the Son, and the Holy Ghost. They think they are smart enough to do it all themselves. They thrive to have the newest, biggest, and best of everything. Material things, drugs, sex, money. They will do whatever it takes, no matter how it goes against God's teachings, to get whatever they want. Things that just last for a moment's pleasure, and it is costing them eternal life. They need to just look at the smallest bird in the sky or the smallest fish in the sea. God provides all of their needs. Birth, life, food, and procreation to carry on. Humans have resorted to killing their own creation, which is God's creation, so that they may have what they want. Worse yet, others are willing to help them do it. More and more are needing help to 'follow this way,' and more and more don't want this help.

"When I was on the beach at Normandy, a great many soldiers were dying as you know. They were far from home, scared, and lonely. They had been thrown into a world they had never imagined. At that time in history, people had more ties to God, and most had been brought up with a religious background. In this far-off land, confusion about all things weighed heavily on them. They were trained to kill. Trained to break a commandment. Some thought that being in a war was a free pass to do other things as well, and God would understand because they were at war. Adultery, theft, everything was okay." Stan was looking into space like he was reliving it as he spoke.

"When the soldiers fell, I was there to help them 'follow this way.' The souls just needed to know that all was not lost. They just need to be reminded that Jesus was waiting for them. The sorrow poured out of those souls, and they were able to travel on with little help. They had once known God, and they had just strayed for a time like lost sheep. The Shepherd welcomed them home."

Zeb listened quietly in awe. He never imagined Stan being in places like the beaches of Normandy. He just always pictured him in hospitals, nursing homes, and maybe accidents like the one he had told about the young child. When he thought about the loss of life that takes place in wars, disasters, and the like, the number of others like Stan who are there to help boggled his mind.

He looked up to ask Stan some more questions, but Stan was gone. He did say that he was getting busier, so he must not have had time to stick around tonight. Zeb could only imagine the things that Stan had seen and the places he had been. He wondered how long Stan had been doing this. The way he was dressed and his hairstyle, Zeb put him in the category of someone from the late eighteen hundreds to the early nineteen hundreds. These were things that would have to wait until the next visit to find out. Hopefully, there would be more visits.

Over the next few weeks, Zeb pondered on what Stan had said. He was getting busier, and the souls didn't want help. The soldiers had been mostly brought up in churches, and their souls only needed a reminder. Those were different times. What has happened to cause the decline in people going to church and getting to know and understand God's teachings? He, himself, had noticed the decline of members in his own congregation. The average age was about sixty-nine. He and Janie were still considered the "young ones." A few young families were attending, but it was nothing like it was thirty years ago. He could remember that when a baby cried or a small child was rambunctious, those in attendance would get annoyed. Today, when this occurs, there are smiles on most faces. It means there is new life in the church, and God is reminding us there is a future, but it is up to us to make sure this future is going in the right direction. It is like the old saying, "It takes a village to raise a child." What can be done to bring people back to God? One way to find out is to ask God, so Zeb prayed for guidance and help to see what was overlooked.

18

The following Sunday, Zeb got up in front of the adult Sunday school class and started to address them. "This week, I would like to go a little off-topic and talk about getting more people to come to church. As I am sure I am not telling you something you don't know, but as you look around the room, we are not getting any younger. Unfortunately, we have lost some members over the last couple of years. We need to try and get some younger people involved and introduce them to Jesus. Let me just say that this is not just a problem in our church but in all churches."

Mrs. Amy Thoms, a fifty-something middle school teacher, was the first to speak. "I think younger people today, and I am saying young adults, not just students, have to adapt to a fast-paced world. They have to have something to constantly hold their attention. Listening to someone preach the Gospel for about thirty minutes just seems to drag on for them. They lose interest, and they go find something that will hold their interest."

John Deets, a local dairy farmer, said, "If there was a Bible video game, I bet they would pay attention to that!"

"That would be a good idea!" said Zeb. "That may even get me into video games!"

Everyone chuckled.

Many ideas were kicked around during the class, and all agreed there were two worth exploring further. The first was to pull out the church membership files and look for those who no longer attended. Church secretary Paula Wilson said she would do this and bring the list to next week's class. They could then divide up the names with the members present, and they would make contact with those who had fallen away. Maybe their reasons for not coming could shed some light on the current problem.

The second idea was to contact other churches and have a meeting together to discuss the lack of attendance. Since it wasn't just a problem in one church, one church shouldn't have to solve it alone. It was agreed to hold the meeting in the church hall two weeks from now and serve some light refreshments. Paula said she would put an invitation letter together and send it to all of the other churches in the area. Several of the women in attendance agreed to make pies. John Deets and Brad Walker said they would make homemade ice cream to go with the pies.

The class ended, and Zeb felt good. This was the first step in bringing the Word of God to the lost sheep and bringing them back to the flock. The churches were going to be working together for the common goal of spreading God's Word.

The two weeks went by quickly, and the multiple church meeting was set for tonight. Zeb and Janie arrived at the church early to unlock the door, get the coffee started, and set up some chairs. They figured if they got twenty to twenty-five people, the meeting was a successful idea.

Mrs. Mary Banks showed up soon after. She was in her sixties and was the perfect image of a rural farmwife coming to a church social. She was about five feet four inches tall, had gray hair in a bun, and was wearing her best apron over her dress and carrying two pies! "Zeb," Mary said, "I am glad you are here. There are two more pies in my car. Would you be kind enough to bring them in for me?"

"I sure will!" Zeb exclaimed. Mrs. Banks was well-known for her pies, and if the meeting was a flop, the pies were still worth showing up for!

As Zeb got to the door, he had to hold it open for Mr. and Mrs. Lukas, who each had two pies a piece. "We sure are going to eat good tonight!" Zeb said as he greeted them. Before the meeting started, eight more pies arrived, and the men showed up with five gallons of homemade ice cream as promised.

When it came time for the meeting to start, more chairs had to be set up, and the total in attendance was fifty-seven. It seems a lot of people have the same goal—to bring others to Jesus. Zeb was smiling from ear to ear. Maybe they can turn things around at least in their small corner of the world. One thing was for sure—HOPE was alive!

Many good ideas were brought up at this meeting, and each congregation picked one to try. Another meeting was scheduled a couple of months out, allowing time to see if there was any success. Each church would bring back its results and share them with the others. The best idea came at the end of the meeting. They all stood and joined in prayer asking for success in bringing people closer to Jesus. Everyone there knew that prayer works!

19

THE CHURCHES CONTINUED TO MEET every few months for the next year to continue to share ideas and pray. Each congregation had seen an increase in attendance. It was not a huge increase, but even just one individual could be considered a victory.

Zeb had just started his evening shift in the boiler room when the tobacco smoke wafted past his nose. In his usual spot sat Stan, puffing on his pipe. "Hello, how are you?" was the greeting, and, "Same, always the same," was the response. "I have some good news for you," reported Zeb. "The local churches have pulled together to try and bring people closer to Jesus, and we are having some success!"

"The Father is pleased," stated Stan.

"Still busy with reluctant souls?" Zeb questioned.

"Yes, very much so," Stan said.

Stan started to speak. "It seems that more young people are passing than the elderly. At least, more young souls needed help to 'follow this way.' It seems that life is no longer a gift to the young. Their lives are ending because they gave in to drug addiction, violence, and sex. All temptations of the evil one. By not knowing Jesus and what He has to offer them, they easily drift toward Satan who is more than willing to help them. He promises them anything they want, but he only grants them one thing—death with eternal damnation.

"I was willed to help the soul of a small child to 'follow this way.' The child's mother was but a child herself. She had given in to the temptation of the flesh, which, in turn, created a new soul. The only love this soul had ever known in its four years of existence was from its mother. She abused, tortured, and despised this child because it had ruined her life. The child asked the mother for something to eat because the child was hungry, and, in a rage, the mother threw the child from a second-story window. As I met the soul, it did not want to leave the battered body. It just wanted to go back to the mother. After all it had been through, it still had love for the mother. When the body became lifeless, the soul came with me, and I led it to 'follow this way.' When I heard the soul cry out, 'Mommy! Mommy!' I knew that the Virgin Mary had accepted it into her arms with endless love and eternal life."

They sat in silence for a moment before Zeb spoke. "Stan, what more can I do?"

"As one person, you are doing as much as you can. You are working tirelessly to spread the Word of God, to bring the lost sheep to the flock. Your greatest strength is through prayer. The Father hears all prayers. If all believers would have the courage to help guide others to heal their souls, my tasks would slow down."

Zeb asked, "Stan, why doesn't God just will all souls to worship Him?"

Stan was hesitant for a moment before he spoke. "God created man in His image, but when the serpent tricked Eve in the garden of Eden, men were given free will. God does not force anyone to do anything. He has offered man eternal life, but in return, you must love Him unconditionally and do His will. Sounds easy, but it is the hardest task known to man. You yourself know how easy it is to fail. If He forced you to love Him, it would be like forcing you into a marriage with someone you don't know or love."

"I never thought of it that way," Zeb commented.

"Blessed are those who know God, know His love, and do His will." After this statement, Stan moved on.

Zeb thought about that statement, *Blessed are those who know God. It is His will that the blessed help the others "follow this way."*

20

The churches kept meeting to try and find new ways to spread the Word of God and to reach more souls. They started to have worship services together and community hymn sings, trying to involve as many interested people as possible. Newcomers and families were joining the congregations of their choice. Some stayed and have become faithful fixtures while others strayed after some time. They were getting the Word of God out to the community, but it was people's choice if they heard it or not.

While eating his lunch one evening at work, Zeb looked up, and Stan was sitting in his usual place. Oddly, there was no smell of pipe tobacco smoke in the air to announce his presence. "Hello, how are you?"

"Same, always the same," was the familiar greeting.

"It has been a while since we spoke. I figured you were busy," Zeb stated.

"Yes, quite busy," Stan said.

After a few moments of silence, Stan started to speak freely. It was like he was trying to get something off his chest, or he was trying to teach Zeb something. "I was willed to an elderly soul that was frightened to leave its body that just no longer could support life. The soul was scared, truly scared. The life it was given was filled with sin. The soul did not know how to repent because it had never known the Father, the Son, and the Holy Ghost. It wasn't even sure if it knew what sin was, but it knew something was not right. That is why it was so scared. It did not know what to do."

"What do you say to the lost souls? Is there a speech that you give?" Zeb questioned.

"No, there are no speeches, no words spoken, at least like you know how to speak with a human voice. When I arrive, there is a promise of hope and the radiance of God's love. This encompasses the soul, and this gives the soul courage to 'follow this way.' However, some souls are still defiant and will not accept God's love. They do not believe. These are the souls that are punished by never getting to enter into eternal life with Jesus."

"If I may ask, what happened to the elderly soul that was scared?" Zeb wanted to know, but maybe it wasn't his place to know.

"It accepted God's love and was set on the path to 'follow this way.' Another lost sheep was found and returned to the flock."

"So that soul found eternal life?" Zeb still wanted a solid answer.

"I have said to you before. My task is to help them 'follow this way.' I am not with them when they meet the Father, the Son, and the Holy Ghost, but if you believe like you say you do, you can draw your own conclusion."

"Stan, how long have you been doing this, helping souls, 'follow this way'?" Zeb questioned him.

"I did it most of my adult life, much in the same way you are doing now."

"No, that is not what I mean," Zeb responded.

"You want to know what happened to me? How did I pass?" Stan asked.

"Yes, if that is not prying too much?"

"No," Stan responded. "I grew up in Belgium, the oldest of four children. My parents ran a small store, and my father taught me the trade. When they got older, and since I was the oldest, I took over the store. And when I married, my wife joined me. We raised two children, a girl and a boy, much like yourself. We were all in the store on August 4, 1914, when the Germans invaded Belgium during WWI. We were all killed in an artillery explosion."

"I am so sorry," Zeb said, almost in a whisper, with his head down.

"Don't be. We all were able to 'follow this way' to eternal life. You cannot even begin to know the magnificence of it."

Zeb's curiosity was starting to get the best of him. "Can I ask you another question? How come you speak perfect English?"

Stan smiled. "God works in mysterious ways. I can communicate with any soul anywhere on earth because it is God's will."

"But you are talking to me, not my soul," Zeb remarked.

"Are you sure?" asked Stan. He smiled and faded away.

Zeb thought about it for a while. *Is Stan really here, or is he in my subconscious? After speaking with him or imagining him, I do work a little harder to bring the Word of God to others. Is he just boosting my soul and not really talking to me and why? Does he just speak to me or others also, or do others like him appear to others like me, and nobody says anything? Am I just crazy?*

21

ZEB WAS STILL BRINGING THE Word of God to as many people as he could through his church. The meetings of all the churches together that had started many years ago had dropped off because many of the older participants passed away. It was rare to find young people coming to church and taking part regularly. If a poll was taken, young people still mostly believed in God, but they just didn't know Him or take time for Him. The churches still filled up on Christmas and Easter, but the rest of the time, things like sports, work, or just downtime took precedence.

When talking to people about the Lord, Zeb had an example that he liked to use that they could maybe relate to and could see themselves. "Say you are in a car accident, what is the first thing that is usually said? 'I hope that I can get my report for work done. I hope we can beat the crosstown rivals in the big game this weekend.' No! Usually, the first thing said is, 'God, help me!' Why should He help you? You have not spoken to Him or visited Him in a long time, but instantly, you want and need His help? What does God do? He helps you in His own way. Maybe not the way you want. Maybe to ease your pain, death comes. Oh, that's bad. That's not what you wanted, but He is giving you a great gift. Another chance at eternal life. How are you prepared to handle it? Do you think it might be easier if you knew Him better? The big game victory may be celebrated for a few hours or a couple of days. How does that compare with the victory of eternal life? That is a victory that you have to practice for every day because you never know when the *coach* is going to call on you!" For some people, this hits home, and it sinks in. Others think they have plenty of time, and they will go to church more when they get older; right now, there is just too much to do.

Zeb was sitting at the boiler room office desk when the phone rang. "Boiler room Zeb Walee," he answered.

"Zeb, this is Stacy Sutton in the ER," said the voice on the other end of the phone. Zeb knew Stacy; she was one of the younger members of his church. She and her husband, Ed, had joined several years ago as a result of the community church meetings. They have four small boys, ages two to eight, who help keep the congregation awake during services. They were good boys, active boys.

"What can I do for you, Stacy?" Zeb asked.

"I don't know if this is right or not, but we have a patient, a young man here in the ER who has been in a bad motorcycle accident. He is asking for a minister to be with him, and we can't get ahold of the hospital chaplain, and you came to my mind. I was hoping that you would be the one to answer the phone. Can you come up?"

"I will be right there, but keep trying the chaplain because I won't be able to stay long," Zeb responded.

Zeb went to the ER and met Stacy who took him into the exam room where the young man was. The man was pretty badly beaten up, but none of his injuries were life-threatening. He was scared and wanted the presence of a minister. "Mr. Marks," Stacy said, "this is Zeb Walee. He works here at the hospital. He is not a minister, but he teaches adult Bible study at my church. I thought you might like to speak with him until the chaplain gets here."

"Okay," he said.

Stacy turned to Zeb and said, "Good luck. I will try the chaplain again."

Zeb walked over to the side of the man's bed; he looked to be about twenty years old with scraggly hair and about a week-old beard. "Mr. Marks, I am Zeb Walee. It looks like you had some bad luck with your motorcycle today."

The young man responded, "My name is Tommy. Yeah, the bike got away from me, but it was no accident. See, my wife told me she was leaving and taking our son with her. I can't stand the thought of not having them in my life, so I was trying to end it all."

"Well, Tommy," Zeb started, "you are still here, which is a gift the Lord has provided you. There is still more for you to do before He calls you home. Now it is up to you to take that gift and find out what He has planned for you. If you don't mind me asking, why does your wife want to leave you?"

"Money," Tommy responded. "We both work but just can't get ahead. Every day is a struggle, and it's tiring. She has just had enough, as have I, but they kept me going, and without them, what's the use."

"Tommy, I don't have all the answers, but I can offer one thing that will help you, and that is prayer. You must believe in God, or you would not have asked for a minister to be with you."

"I do," said Tommy, choking back tears. "I know suicide is wrong, and I am afraid God will be mad at me."

"Tommy, Tommy, God loves you. Your judgment was just clouded by the thought of losing your family. He gave you a second chance to make things right. You have to trust Him. I, too, almost lost someone dear to me in this very ER many years ago. I turned my fear to anger against Him. Once my judgment was clear, I could see He gave me a second chance also. Let's pray together, Tommy. Dear Jesus, I have stumbled, and I ask that You pick me up in Your arms and give me strength and guidance to accept Your will. Jesus, I ask You to keep my family together like your holy family. Amen."

When they finished, they realized that Stacy had entered the room. "Mr. Marks," she said, "your wife is here. Would you like me to bring her back to be with you?"

"Yes," Tommy said.

"Tommy, I have to go back to work now, but I will make sure the nurse gives you my number in case you ever need it, but I think you will be okay. Remember, God will give you everything you need when you need it, and it is not always money." Zeb turned to leave the room just as Mrs. Marks was entering, and he smiled at her as he left.

Zeb waited at the nurse's station for Stacy. "Here is my phone number. Would you make sure Mr. Marks gets it before he leaves?"

"I will," said Stacy, and she hugged him tightly. "I am glad you were here because you just saved him like you saved Ed and me."

22

Zeb went back to the boiler room office feeling good and rejuvenated, hoping he had helped Tommy Marks and knowing that he had helped Ed and Stacy Sutton. It's not often that you get to see the results firsthand of doing God's work!

Almost a year had passed, and again Zeb was in the boiler room office. He caught the strong smell of pipe tobacco smoke. In his usual chair sat Stan. The conversation started the same as it had in those many years Stan had been visiting. "Hello, how are you?"

"Same, always the same."

Zeb didn't want to pat himself on the back, but he couldn't wait to tell Stan how he helped Tommy Marks through a rough time and how he helped get Ed and Stacy Sutton back to the flock.

Stan didn't say anything for a few moments, maybe to let Zeb's pride settle down. "Your work in spreading God's Word makes a difference, but it is not you doing the work. It is God's will working through you. You must remember that God's hand is in everything. You don't always know how it works out, but if one person learns the teachings of God and, in turn, spread the teachings to one person and so on, eventually, His Word spreads. It is not up to just the ministers, pastors, priests, and the like. It is up to everyone. Everyone does not have to be a biblical scholar and great orator. A kind word, a small gesture, or an act of kindness is all God's work. 'When you do it for the least of My brothers, you do it for Me.'" Stan encouraged Zeb with these words.

"Stan," Zeb asked, "did you study religion in Belgium?"

There was a pause before Stan spoke. "My parents were very religious, and we attended church as often as we could. Every night, my father would read to us from the Bible as we sat by the fire. He was very intelligent, and as he read to us, he would explain it so that we could understand the lesson. My father did well in business because he was fair and generous, and the people knew it. When they could not afford the necessities of life, he would make sure they still received them. When they were sick, he made sure they had medicine. His business never suffered from the lack of payment. He stated many times, 'God will give me what I need when I need it, and I am thankful that He doesn't give me what I truly deserve.'"

Zeb questioned, "What does that mean, *Give me what I deserve?* For his kind ways, was he not blessed with a good family and a successful business?"

"Yes," responded Stan, "we were all blessed. My father, like all, was a human, and he knew that he was stained by sin, and what he deserved was God's punishment, but it didn't happen because of the love and forgiveness of the Father."

It now made sense to Zeb. Stan's father was doing God's will in the way God had directed him, and God was pleased. He went to speak and noticed that Stan was gone.

Zeb reflected on his own life. He had always been healthy. He had a wonderful wife who had been by his side since they were kids. He had two children who are now successful in life, raising their own children with God's teachings. He has always had a good job at Mercy General Hospital and was able to provide for his family. Most of all, he knew God, and he trusted Jesus, and this is why he is blessed.

23

Zeb didn't know that would be the last time he would see or talk to Stan. The following year, Zeb retired from the boiler room at Mercy General Hospital after forty-two years of service, and Stan never appeared to him anywhere else. Janie retired that year after a successful career of teaching and guiding young minds.

Their retirement was going to be just relaxing, traveling, and watching their grandchildren grow up. This was all right for the first several months, but it wasn't their passion. They felt that since they had more free time, it should be used more in doing God's work. They had to have a plan, so they prayed for guidance.

It was just a few days when their phone rang. It was the secretary from a church across town inviting them to a community meeting about starting a food and clothing pantry for those in need. Janie told her that they were very interested and that they would be there. Once again, prayer was the answer, and God was guiding them to do His will.

The night of the meeting came, and there were a lot of familiar faces in the crowd of about twenty. They all greeted one another and introduced themselves to those they did not know. It was about time for the meeting to start, so they all took a seat.

The young minister walked up from the back of the room. "Hello, how are you? I would like to thank you all for coming. For those of you who don't know me, I am Pastor Thomas Marks, better known as Pastor Tommy."

Zeb was a little puzzled. Could this be the Tommy Marks he spoke with in the ER several years ago? The voice sounded familiar, but he looked nothing like the young man lying on that hospital bed thinking his life was over. Pastor Tommy was clean-shaven with short hair and was a little heavier.

The meeting ended, and Zeb heard very little after the words *Pastor Tommy*. When most of the attendees left, Zeb made his way over to Pastor Tommy. "Pastor Tommy, did you used to have a motorcycle?"

Pastor Tommy looked at Zeb and, after a couple of seconds, recognized him and threw his arms around him. It was the same Tommy Marks. Zeb introduced Janie to him and reminded her of the story of how he helped a young man in the ER when the chaplain wasn't available. Pastor Tommy called his wife over to introduce her. "Mr. Walee, this is my wife, Ashley. You met her in the ER that day."

She also threw her arms around Zeb and hugged him tightly. "Mr. Walee, you saved my husband's life and our marriage. Thank you! When I met you that day, I had a feeling of hope and love coming over me. It is hard to explain, but I knew everything would be okay."

They talked for about an hour about how Tommy's life changed that day in the hospital. Pastor Tommy commented that Zeb's presence helped him 'follow His way.' When he said that, Zeb had an odd feeling come over him. Good, but odd. He also remembered the greeting Pastor Tommy gave to the group tonight, *Hello, how are you?* Was Stan letting him know that he was still there?

Pastor Tommy and Ashley became a big part of Zeb's and Janie's lives. They, along with others, brought the food and clothing pantry to life and made it a success. On the days they were not there, Zeb and Janie visited hospitals, nursing homes, and shut-ins bringing the Word of God to as many people as possible.

As time moved on, it became apparent that they could no longer keep up as they once did. Their lives were slowing down, and eventually, they became residents of a nursing home themselves. They shared a room so they would still be together, and they were still spreading God's Word to the other residents on the days they were able.

One night, Zeb was dreaming, and in his dream, he smelled the sweet aroma of pipe tobacco smoke, and he saw Stan. "Hello, how are you?"

"Same, always the same."

Zeb felt good, young, with no aches or pains; this was a good dream. Stan spoke. "Follow this way."

Zeb then realized that it was not a dream. Stan was there to take him *home*, but he fought it. "I can't leave Janie!" Zeb's soul shouted.

At that second, Janie's voice whispered, "Zeb, it is all right. I am going with you."

That night, they both passed peacefully—the way they lived—together.

There was a framed saying that always hung on the wall of their home. Rose and Jimmy thought it appropriate to have it carved on their tombstone.

> WE ARE ALL BUT A WINDOW FOR
> GOD'S LOVE TO SHINE THROUGH.

ABOUT THE AUTHOR

THE AUTHOR WAS RAISED ON a small farm in West Virginia. He was the youngest of six children growing up in a very devout Catholic family. After high school, he chose not to further his academic education but go right into the industrial workforce. He got a job in an oil refinery where his father had retired from, and he worked his way into the boiler house and eventually became a full-time boiler operator. He has finished his boiler career working in the boiler room of a local hospital. He continues, to this day, to be very devoted to his religion along with his own family. With his wife and daughter, they still continue to run a small farm, sharing the fruits of their labor with those around them. The idea for this book came from working in the hospital and some of the experiences he had while there. His goal as an author is to help spread the Word of God and to help people realize there will always be hope.

www.ingramcontent.com/pod-product-compliance
Lightning Source LLC
Chambersburg PA
CBHW022101150726
47990CB00003B/1197

9 7 9 8 8 8 8 9 4 3 1 5 4 1